Art in Nature

Previous page

Bluebells in Cotchford Wood   Caryl J Mann

Inspired by a bluebell wood that has been destroyed and lost forever. Dark, vibrant blues and greens were used to establish the structure of the painting. The light areas were built up using layer after layer of small brush strokes, with tonal values and detail slowly added to capture the quality of the light on the landscape.

Acrylic: 458 x 355mm (18 x 14in).

Opposite

Woodland Harvest   Catherine Ann Harrison

Inspired by the many varieties of fungi found in a local woodland. Because the fresh colours and textures of fungi deteriorate very rapidly once they are picked, a still life was set up and photographed. An accurate drawing was made using the photograph as reference and colour washes built up over the drawn image. As the paper dried more detail was added with a much drier brush.

Watercolour and gouache:
500 x 350mm (20 x 14in).

Page 4

Gulls and Oystercatchers   Jon Dudley

Inspired by the contrasting scale and movement of great black-backed gulls and oystercatchers. Following the composition, a monoprint process was used by covering a board with oil paint, placing wall paper on to the inked surface, and drawing the image which appeared in reverse overleaf. Tone was added by applying pressure to the areas required and mistakes corrected by gluing paper and reprinting. The drawing was strengthened with charcoal and painted using watercolour with wax resist.

Monoprint, charcoal, watercolour and wax :
1100 x 480mm (44 x 19$^{1}/_{4}$in).

ART IN NATURE

Inspiration from the natural world

SEARCH PRESS

Contents

Foreword

In 1992 I felt that there was a need for a competition and exhibition to celebrate the inspiration artists find in the natural world, and to encourage them to search for new directions by exploring different approaches to the subject through the use of traditional or more contemporary materials and methods. The Society for Wildlife Art of the Nations (SWAN) responded by agreeing to house an exhibition of works selected from the competition. Chevron agreed to offer a prestigious £3,000 first purchase prize, art materials companies supported the idea by awarding many additional prizes, and in many cases the chosen work offered new ideas and inspiration to other artists.

This year, to celebrate the fourth year of the Art in Nature competition and exhibition, Search Press agreed to publish this wonderful selection of prize-winning, exhibited and other celebratory works from the competition. The artists explain how they have interpreted their ideas, to stimulate and help you to decide what kind of approach or subject matter to explore in your own work.

I hope this beautiful book will inspire and delight you, and I wish you much enjoyment with your art.

Dr Sally Bulgin
Editor, *The Artist magazine.*

Marsh Life   Justin Hindley

Inspired by the dense, lush growth of the watery valleys of Cornwall in England. Gum arabic was added to the paints to enrich the pigments and to give a glaze to the paint. Keeping the brush work simple, fresh and direct, colour was washed on to watercolour paper. Using stiff hogs hair brushes, adjustments were made, cutting through the pigment to the white of the paper.

Watercolour and gum arabic:
1200 x 790mm (48 x 31¹/₂in).

THE ROYAL SOVEREIGN/TALENS AWARD

Watercolours and gouache

Snow on the Tops   Bernard Atherton

Inspired by a walk in the snow. Attempts to paint on site failed when the first brush full of colour froze on contact with the paper. The painting was based on colour notes and drawings, and was completed at home. The sky was washed in and allowed to dry before building up the distance and middle distance. Finally, the rocks and purple shadows were added, which emphasized the soft texture and crispy whiteness of the snow.

Watercolour: 318 x 206mm (12³/₄ x 8¹/₄in).

THE WINSOR AND NEWTON AWARD

Opposite

The National Park, Spain - Province of Seville   Daphne Beak Alexander

Inspired by the artist's holiday experiences. Working wet-into-wet with a pastry brush, cobalt blue was applied round the clouds and mountains, with touches of payne's grey on the horizon. The mountains and foreground were defined with ultramarine blue, then local colours applied. The painting was allowed to dry before shadows and details were added.

Watercolour: 475 x 350mm (19 x 14in).

Above

Promenade Beach, South Coast of Australia   Hilary S Burnett

Inspired by the deep rich colours of the sea and rocks, and the 'freedom' of the waves. The sky was washed in over an accurate pencil sketch, and later airbrushed with a film of white gouache to create distance. The sea was washed in using Prussian blue, ultramarine blue and viridian, combined with touches of alizaron crimson. White gouache was used to enhance the waves and foam. The rocks were built up in a jigsaw style with layers of washes to produce the required texture.

Watercolour and gouache: 675 x 450mm (27 x 18in).

Mount Tarawera, Rotarua, New Zealand   Clifford Bayly

Inspired by a helicopter trip over one of the most impressive volcanoes on the North Island. It was impossible to paint this on location, so the painting was worked up back in the studio using photographs, drawn notes and a good memory – which was heightened by the drama of the situation. Excitement and contrast were created by using cool greys for the larger areas to complement the reds and yellow in the crater. Pigment was applied fairly dry to gain texture from the paper.

Watercolour: 725 x 475mm (29 x 19in).

Franz Joseph Glacier to Rain Forest, New Zealand   Clifford Bayly

Inspired by the contrasts of the awesome mass of the glacier against the black mountains the feathery tree ferns in the valley. This was painted in the studio using location studies. A carefully integrated tonal composition was prepared. Initially wet-into-wet was used for the cloud forms. A 50mm (2in) flat brush was used for the principal forms, and a smaller brush for the vegetation and the foreground detail. A limited palette was used to reflect the cool, wet nature of the subject.

Watercolour: 475 x 700mm (19 x 28in).

Common Terns
James Bartholomew

Inspired by the English Hebridean coast and its wildlife. After several days of sketching and watching the bird life on Skye's coast, a composition was compiled from the various references. Many overlapping washes of gouache were used to build up a highly active and changing sea surface. Pastel was wetted and moved around with the paint. The marks were applied in a harsh and aggressive way to suggest the hostility of the environment.

Watercolour and pastel:
720 x 400mm (28³/4 x 16in).

Black-tailed Godwits   Linda Gaffey

Inspired by unusual numbers of black tailed godwits visiting Frodsham in Cheshire, England. Sketches were drawn and photographs taken on location. These were used as reference back in the studio. A pencil outline was drawn on to tinted watercolour paper, and a loose wash of Payne's grey and raw sienna was flooded in for the water. The birds were painted in using alizaron crimson, French ultramarine, burnt umber and cadmium yellow. Highlights were added using white gouache.

Watercolour and gouache: 675 x 475mm (27 x 19in).

Roseate Terns – Memory   Philip Snow

Inspired by memories and many sketches of terns 'dancing' over the clear turquoise waters of Wales and Scotland. Sketches from life were enlarged on to watercolour paper. The sandy sea bed was painted in quickly around the terns, allowed to dry and then washed over with a mixture of cerulean blue, cobalt blue and terre verte. The terns were painted in as shadows, a few details added, and then darker ripples added to the sea. Tonal adjustments were made to the terns and finally the sea shadows were painted on to their bodies.

Watercolour: 350 x 225mm (14 x 9in).

North Shore, Iona, Scotland
Anthony Bailey

Inspired by the light and colour found on the island of Iona. The sky was washed straight on to watercolour paper, without an initial drawing. The distant hills were painted in before adding the sea and the middle distance. The foreground was washed in loosely and finally the darker rocks were added. This picture was painted on location.

Watercolour:
355 x 210mm (14 x 8¹/₄in).

Razorbills in strong morning sunshine Barden Island 16/6/97

Darren Woodhead.

Razorbills Bardsey Island 15/6/99. warm clear + sunny. again!!!

Razorbills in Sun – Bardsey Island   Darren Woodhead

Inspired by the birds and the will to draw and paint them in their natural habitat. A number of drawings were made on the spot so that the razorbills could be painted with confidence. This small group was selected, quickly drawn on to watercolour paper and then colour added, building up tones, texture and shadows.

Watercolour: 420 x 297mm (16³⁄₄ x 11³⁄₄in).

Opposite

Razorbills Against Strong Lit Rocks   Darren Woodhead

Inspired by razorbills beautifully camouflaged against sunlit rocks. This group was drawn quickly in pencil before adding colour. The shadows and colours of the birds were painted first on to watercolour paper to capture them naturally in their rocky habitat.

Watercolour: 297 x 420mm (11³⁄₄ x 16³⁄₄in).

Chinese Quail James Williamson-Bell

Inspired by a long interest in wildlife and Chinese painting. Traditional Chinese materials
have been used and the ink is a mixture of bottled and ground stick ink. The style of the
painting is 'Xie yi' which aims at capturing the spirit of the subject, rather than its fine detail.
Watercolour is washed on to the paper, with splashes of the same colour added to the
background. The birds and detail are painted in using contrasting ink colours.

Watercolour and Chinese ink: 400 x 325mm (16 x 13in).

THE ST CUTHBERTS PAPER MILL PURCHASE PRIZE

Opposite

Quiet Corner, Nene Karl Taylor

Inspired by the plant texture, colour and mood. The Nene was roughly drawn in. The
background was painted in first with a mix of burnt sienna, burnt umber and a touch of
cadmium red, and the colours were then built up from light to dark. Wax resist was applied
before the colour washes to create areas of white. Finally the Nene was painted in and then
the foreground.

Watercolour and wax resist: 500 x 675mm (20 x 27in).

A Quiet Place   Eve Foster

Inspired by alternating patches of light and dark. After observing the scene over several days at the same time each day, the main blocks of tone were planned and placed, using weak cobalt. Leaving areas of white paper for the whites, the painting was built up from light to dark. The final picture was rather dark, so a few highlights were scratched out and spots of orange and purple added.

Watercolour: 231 x 337mm (9¼ x 13½in).

18

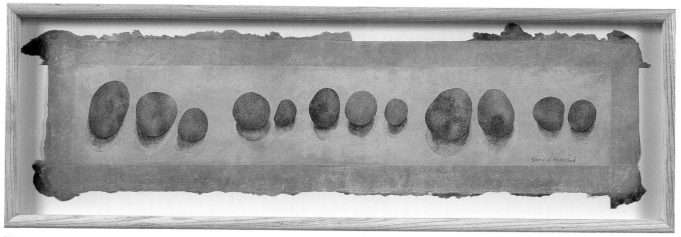

Chesil Tara Syeda Hansford

Inspired by the artist's affinity with the Dorset landscape and her love of the natural features that compose our stunning landscapes. The three separate paintings show collections of pebbles from Abbotsbury beach. The jewel-like quality and individuality of the pebbles has been captured on a surface of coffee mixed with emulsion paints. Gouache is applied directly to this surface and the colours carefully built up.

Gouache, coffee, emulsion paints and sea water:
700 x 750mm (28 x 30in).

THE DALER-ROWNEY AWARD

Visiting the garden shed   Toni Hargreaves

Inspired by a shed which had been undisturbed for over ten years, and which nature was beginning to claim for herself. Using photographs taken on location as reference, the composition was worked up on tracing paper. The sparrow was deliberately positioned so that its presence was not immediately apparent. Once the composition was acceptable the drawing was transferred and the colours applied, working from the top of the painting downwards. The yellow of the tin was emphasised, making it the focal point, evoking a sense of warmth and nostalgia. The wall and the area under the shelf needed to be much darker, and they were airbrushed to avoid disturbing the paint underneath. Finally, the sparrow was painted in, completing the picture.

Gouache: 350 x 250mm (14 x 10in).

The Creek in Autumn   Ginnie de Vroomen

Inspired by the transformation of a much-loved area by the fiery colours of autumn.
Preliminary watercolour sketches were made on location to explore different ways of
conveying rhythms and patterns within the trees and fallen leaves, and to experiment with
the intensity of the colour contrasts. These sketches provided reference back in the studio.
The main features were sketched in and washes laid in on watercolour paper to establish the
colour areas. Detail was formed using wet-into-wet and wet-on-dry where appropriate. The
translucency of the paint was essential to convey the light glowing through the leaves.

Watercolour: 420 x 590mm (16³/₄ x 23¹/₂in).

Acrylics

Hoopoe   Karl Taylor

Inspired by the texture of the roof timbers and the combination of colours. Using a decorating brush, the sky was roughed in, then the roof was blocked in using a mixture of Payne's grey and burnt umber. When the painting was dry, colour was built up by overpainting and glazing, until the desired result was achieved. Trying to get the illusion of grass on the roof without too much detail was difficult, but fun. Final details were then added.

Acrylic: 725 x 625mm (29 x 25in).

Daisies in the morning   Caryl Mann

Inspired by warm early morning light which gave the field of daisies a strange luminosity.
The intense blue of the shadows were painted in and built up to contrast with the soft light
warmth of the foreground. Unbleached titanium white and cadmium orange were applied
in small key brush strokes and used for glazing throughout the painting process.

Acrylic: 458 x 355mm (18 x 14in).

Root Forms   Martin Turner

Inspired by the interesting movements and textures of exposed tree roots in a sandy soil. This picture was painted on mounting board and textures were built up using areas of sandpaper which were glued to the surface. These areas were then brushed over with a fairly dry, loaded colour. Other areas were painted quite thinly, or glazed, to obtain contrasting textures.

Acrylic: 1000 x 750mm (40 x 30in).

THE LIQUITEX ACRYLIC AWARD

Right

Grasses – Dartmoor Janet McCulloch

Inspired by a man-made rock circle overgrown with long grass. Using rough, unstretched watercolour paper pinned to a board, the grass was washed in thinly. Colour was occasionally lifted off with a watercolour brush handle tip and the blades of grass were then drawn in with oil crayon. The rocks were painted with layers of transparent glazes, using acrylic medium to thin the paint.

Acrylic and oil crayon: 562 x 750mm (22 1/2 x 30in).

Below

Between Storms, Brotherswater Alison Spratt

Inspired by interesting light effects just after a storm while backpacking in Cumbria, England. Using location sketches as reference, the image was quickly drawn with paint on to the canvas back in the studio. The main colours were loosely brushed on and built up in layers. Edges were sharply defined with a small brush. The work was completed in only a few hours.

Acrylic: 915 x 610mm (36 1/2 x 24 1/2in).

North Sea No:1
Sandra Bright

Inspired by the reflection of light on water and fish. Heavy watercolour paper was stapled to a board. Keeping the fish images dry, clean water was flooded on to the surface. Washes were dropped and splashed at random over the whole area and darker tones were then built up using more washes. Finally, the fish were painted in when the surface was barely damp.

Acrylic:
750 x 1062mm (30 x 42 1/2in).

Opposite
School No: 2 – Migration   Sandra Bright

Inspired by the movement of water and fish. Firstly the fish were masked out and a light wash of acrylic was applied over the whole surface. This was then textured with cling film. When the paint was dry darker tones were added and selected areas were lifted using a stiff brush. The masking was removed and the fish painted in. Finally, more texture was added to the water using a brush.

Acrylic: 750 x 1062mm (30 x 42 1/2in).

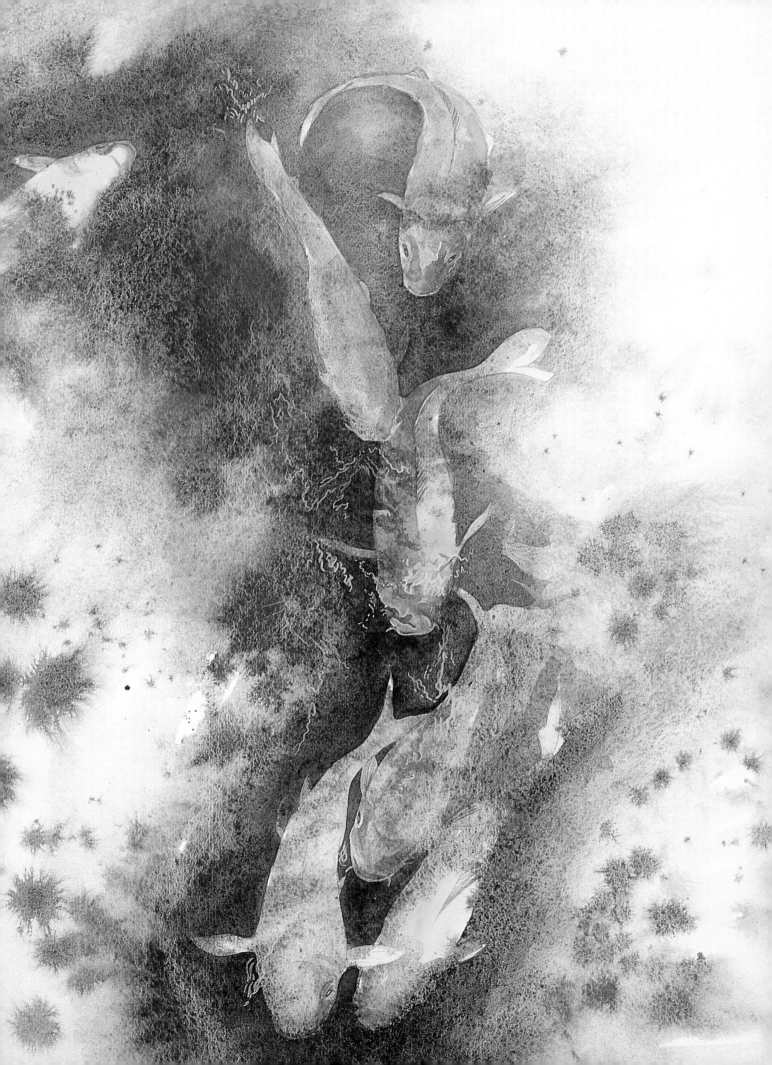

Oils

The Common Blue Butterfly   Richard Tratt

Inspired by the long hot English summer of 1995. Sketches were made on location. Back in the studio basic areas of sunlight and shadow were laid on to the canvas. A glazing/scumbling technique was used with a mix of raw sienna, burnt umber and a selection of blues. The butterfly's position was then marked. The painting was allowed to dry and was finished on location using hog brushes and a long hair brush for the tall grasses.

Oil: 1000 x 900mm (40 x 36in).

THE CHEVRON FIRST PURCHASE PRIZE

Brambles Barry A Peckham

Inspired by the backlit effect of sun on dew soaked leaves. The painting was completed on location using a primed, stained acrylic canvas. Diluted paint was used to indicate the main features, before vigorously laying on the shadow areas. The painting was established in the first session by gradually building up the lighter areas. The initial work was refined in subsequent sessions and final subtleties added.

Oil: 750 x 700mm (30 x 28in).

Evening Light Patricia Clarke

Inspired by the light, colour and wildness of the English landscape glimpsed later on an autumn day. This is a *plein air*, *alla prima* oil painting with a high eye level. It was painted quickly on to prepared canvas using a limited palette, big brushes and a painting knife. The optimum viewpoint was selected and the house positioned very carefully on the canvas. A zig-zag pattern was looked for to lead the eye into the painting and the birch trees were used as essential verticals.

Oil: 600 x 500mm (24 x 20in).

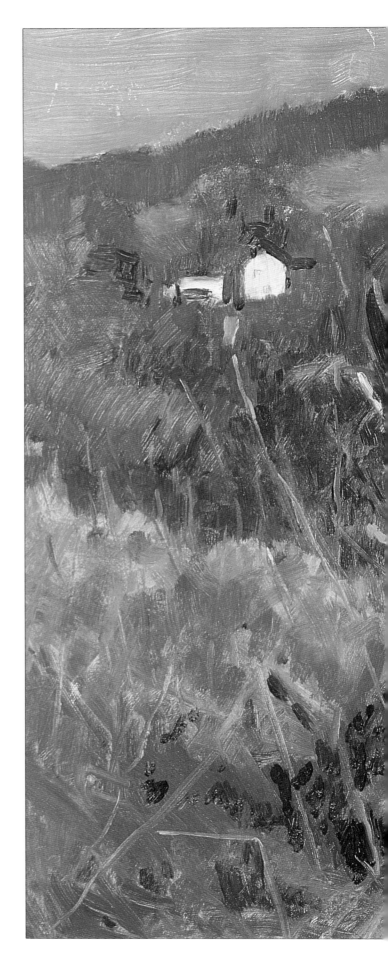

Thoughtless of Me   Geoff Stalker

Inspired by a ditch near the artist's studio. The paintings above and opposite are purely a sensory response to what the artist sees. He tries to eliminate thought, concept and idea from his work and to this end paints things at the bottom end of the ecological ladder: mud, decaying vegetable matter, unidentifiable weeds. He then paints these subjects as he sees them. Both paintings are worked on canvas. A variety of mediums are used to build up the paint in layers. Glazes are used over discordant colours to intensify and enhance the colours.

Oil: 900 x 1200mm (36 x 48in).

Opposite

Bitten   Geoff Stalker

Inspired by the Rio Grande Valley, Colorado, America. This painting is of a snake infested mosquito farm high up in the Rockies – but this was of no importance. The light, the heat, the rhythm of the reeds and the way the pools intensified the reflected colours of the sky and vegetation were important.

Oil: 850 x 1200mm (34 x 48in).

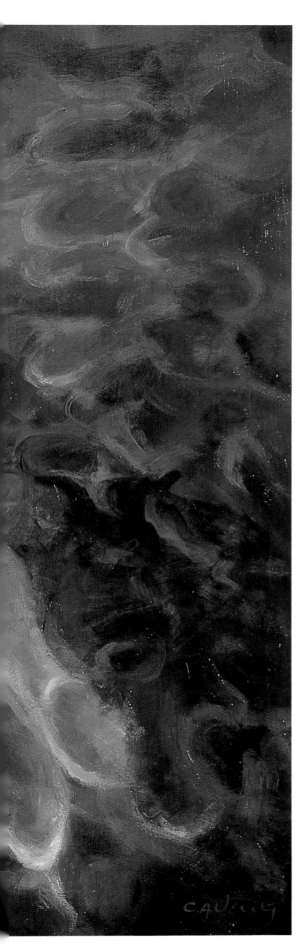

Green Turtles, Great Barrier Reef, Australia   Claire Verity

Both paintings were inspired by an Australian visit where the artist was lucky enough to swim amongst these beautiful green turtles. She was so inspired by the colours and patterns on their shells, she had to paint them. The grace and nobility of the turtles and the exquisite colours were captured with the aid of an underwater camera. With the aid of the photographs, sketches and notes, the depth and translucency of colour were carefully built up on the canvas. In the painting above the shape of the turtle's amber green carapace echoed the shapes of the coral beds. Both paintings are the same size.

Oil: 750 x 600mm (30 x 24in).

Silage Grass
Gareth Brown

Inspired by the colours and textures of silage grass blown from farm trucks. Areas of silage grass were photographed at close range. The paint was applied directly on to a primed board covered with a thin ground of oil colour, without any draft work. Colours, texture and depth were enhanced and finished as the painting progressed.

Oil:
750 x 538mm (30 x 21¹/₂in).

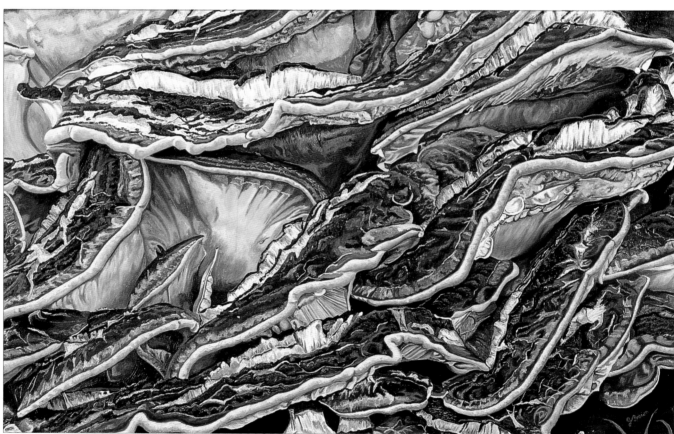

Bracket Fungi II   Gareth Brown

Inspired by the almost abstract quality of the structure within the bracket fungi when it was closely observed. Photographs were taken and subjects painstakingly selected for the composition. Only those shapes, colours and textures which inspired an image were chosen. A board was carefully prepared and the picture drafted out, then the painting was worked up with all its fine detail.

Oil: 750 x 500mm (30 x 20in).

Bank   Michael Garton

Inspired by a broken branch held in suspension. This was painted entirely on location, using a direct oil painting technique on canvas, and a wide angle of vision was taken, in response to the 'wrap round' feeling of life. The transition between earth and sky in the forest was an important element in the composition – the tops of the trees stretching towards the infinity of space, and the earth-bound roots towards the centre of matter.

Oil: 645 x 545mm (25³/₄ x 21³/₄in).

Pastels

Water Meadows
Brian Lindley

Inspired by the quiet beauty of the wetlands of Norfolk, England. Pencil sketches and colour notes were made on location. These were used as reference back in the studio. Adjustments were made to the initial drawing before transferring the design to the paper. This was then blocked in with dark and light tones, followed by middle tones. The colours and tones were adjusted throughout the painting process with highlights added right at the end.

Pastel: 350 x 225mm (14 x 9in).

40

River Light Colin Allbrook

Inspired by the sun and the changing light on the river below the artist's house. Several watercolour studies were made on location. These were used as reference while planning the pastel painting in the studio. The main areas were established on dark green board, by lightly laying in the composition with compressed charcoal. The colours were gradually built up with soft pastel and strengthened as the painting developed.

Pastel: 500 x 325mm (20 x 13in).

Opposite (above)

The Summit of Ben Nevis Jonathan Taylor

Inspired by the contrast between the stoney summit and the atmospheric, hazy depth. Watercolour was used to block in the composition, establishing tone values which helped create a sense of space. The painting was then worked up with pastel. Different application methods were used – blending with fingers, letting the brush strokes show through and using them directly to give a more textured finish.

Pastel and watercolour: 520 x 350mm (20³/₄ x 14in).

Opposite (below)

Coire Nan Arr, Scotland Jonathan Taylor

Inspired by the drama and wildness of the scene. This was originally sketched one very wet day, after a night of heavy rain. The final composition was roughed in using watercolour, to establish the tones and base colour. Pastel was then used to create a sense of 'weather'. The foreground texture had to be controlled otherwise the picture would have become too fussy.

Pastel and watercolour: 535 x 365mm (21¹/₂ x 14¹/₂in).

Drawing

Sunset at Caesar's Camp   Martin Bright

Inspired by a blinding sunset flooding through trees, seen from within a hollow. A drawing was made on the spot with soft pencil, noting the tonal patterns. Using this as reference, mixed media drawings were made in the studio. Starting with watercolour washes, the picture was built up using a soft pencil and crayon. Finally, white acrylic was used to bring back the strongest white possible.

Pencil, crayon, watercolour and acrylic: 925 x 675mm (37 x 27in).

THE REXEL DERWENT DRAWING AWARD

Opposite

Anglesey Rocks   Beverley Mason

Inspired by the dynamic, brutal coastline of Anglesey in winter. The main areas of tone were loosely blocked in with charcoal. The weight and solidity of the rocks was captured by layering the image, fixing it after each stage. Drawing with line, the charcoal was dragged using a fine grade sandpaper, reinforcing the direction of the rock formations, but at the same time keeping their definition.

Charcoal and chalk: 594 x 840mm (23³/₄ x 33¹/₂in).

Winter Hedgerow
Janet Perrior

Inspired by the artist's interest in the rhythms and patterns of nature which can be seen when focusing on small, detailed areas. After sketching in the main lines of the drawing, and using various grades of graphite pencil, the picture was worked from the top left-hand corner across the paper in bands to the right-hand edge. This was repeated, then specific areas were worked on to organise the composition into a totally coherent visual image.

Pencil:
200 x 275mm (8 x 11in).

Opposite

Young Bracken   Justin Hindley

Inspired by the sight of bracken fronds emerging from the earth in early spring, spreading like an army of plant warriors. The paper was prepared with a ground of gesso rolled on quite thickly to create a strong surface with a texture. The image was created using compressed charcoal which was later manipulated with erasers, drawn and moulded and redrawn. Finally, some white acrylic paint was used. The drawing was sprayed with fixative, which not only served to secure the image, but seemed to enrich it with a slight glaze.

Compressed charcoal and acrylic: 580 x 850mm (23¹/₄ x 34in).

Claire Harkess '16

Mixed media and collage

Music Hall Pigeons   Claire Harkess

Inspired by daily pavement encounters with town pigeons. The inclusion of collage not only helped to add structure and texture, but it also helped to symbolise the function of the hall. The images were built up in loose layers, splattering the colours, and the drawing was tightened up in parts until the artist was satisfied with the picture and the way it looked.

Watercolour and collage: 650 x 488mm (26 x 19¹/₂in).

Below

Red-breasted Goose   David Cook

Inspired by the abstract shapes contained within a natural form. The simplified shapes and colours were drawn on to thin tracing paper. This was laid over brown textured paper and cut through with a scalpel. Blue-grey paper was laid under the brown paper when the beak was cut. The tracing was laid on burnt sienna paper and the remaining shapes cut. Finally, the pieces of paper were glued on to a cream textured paper.

Textured paper: 200 x 200mm (8 x 8in).

Above

Shelducks Migrating   James Bartholomew

Inspired by shelducks flying south over the Scottish highland lochs. Like the flight of the birds, the scene was quiet and calm. The skyscape was painted first using a mixture of gouache and pastel mixed together with water. It was soft-edged so as not to distract attention from the subject. The birds were painted with a mixture of gouache and wet pastel and were treated with minimum detail to retain a loose feel.

Gouache and pastel: 500 x 300mm (20 x 12in).

Massa Cararra   Millie Bridge

Inspired by holidays in Tuscany, Italy. The subject was drawn accurately and then alternative compositions were worked out. Having chosen the most pleasing composition, watercolour was washed over the background area and cling film placed over the wet colour. This was lifted off when the paint was dry, to create an interesting textured surface. Handmade papers, tissues and magazine pages were torn and cut, and glued down, superimposing the shapes until the composition was complete. Finally, the picture was covered with glue and a little water as a varnish, to keep the colours and patterns from fading.

Watercolour and paper collage: 500 x 450mm (20 x 18in).

Opposite

Lesser Black-backed Gulls   Nik Pollard

Inspired by the gulls and the simple composition, which was intensified by the strength of the light on the birds. The painting was worked up from an initial field study. The staleness of duplication was avoided by working freely with charcoal and watercolour. The sketch was recaptured in a fresh way by concentrating on impression, rather than realism.

Watercolour and charcoal: 875 x 500mm (35 x 20in).

The Steadfast Oak (Homage to Capricorn)   Julie Abrahams

Inspired by the artist's interest in astrology and her awe of the natural world, the painting
personifies the main characteristics of those born under the sign of Capricorn. Paint was
applied over a charcoal drawing. Form and texture were carefully built up using layers of
hand-made paper. Leaves were pressed into the newly made damp paper; they were then cut
out and applied to the collage. By using more natural materials and leaf embossments the
finished result has a very natural feel.

Hand-made papers, charcoal and acrylics: 1450 x 1400mm (58 x 56in).

Autumn Tree   Jill Mackie

Inspired by the afternoon light falling on the artist's pear tree which was full of ripe fruit. Kitchen foil and magazine paper were glued down in broad tonal areas. Coloured tissue papers were then used to enhance the design and to get a sense of the subject. The image was built up using paper, inks and oil pastel. Finally, layers of re-touching varnish were added to the picture. This rendered the tissue semi-transparent, revealing layers of underlying colour and tone.

Paper, ink, oil pastel and varnish: 525 x 400mm (21 x 16in).

Under the Waves   Lola Dyke

This collage was worked in concentrated watercolours and dyes on a paper support. A
painting was made and while this was still very wet, a print was taken in creased tissue paper.
When dry, the printed images were separated and the tissue was rearranged on top of the
original painting, tearing where necessary. It was then glued into place. Finally, some areas
of colour were lifted with diluted bleach.

Watercolour, dyes and tissue paper: 550 x 600mm (22 x 24in).

Opposite

Eretmochelys Imbritica 'Hawksbill Turtles'   Cathryn Gilbert

Inspired by the plight of the Loggerhead turtles in Zakynthos, Greece. Studies of the turtles
were made at London Zoo. They were initially drawn in water-soluble graphite pencil. The
remainder of the painting was worked up while the paper was wet, to create a water effect.
Starting with washes, the artist worked in pools of pigment using a large brush and a sponge.
Watercolour pencils were then used to enhance the turtles. Once the whole image was dry,
colour tones were deepened and more detail added with charcoal.

Water-soluble graphite pencil, watercolour, watercolour pencils and charcoal:
775 x 1050mm (31 x 42in).

THE SIR PETER SCOTT MEMORIAL PRIZE

Dragonfly   Simon Hervey Haycraft

Inspired by the unusual lighting over the Rhododendrons which caused highlights and shadows to fall on the rocks and water. The rocks above the surface of the water were drawn on to watercolour paper with oil pastel. Watercolour was used to loosely paint in the stream. Detail was added to the foliage with a mixture of acrylic, gouache and watercolour. The different media enabled the artist to separate rocks, water and foliage, giving each its own quality. The dragonfly was added to symbolise the moment.

Oil pastel, acrylic, gouache and watercolour: 650 x 550mm (26 x 22in).

Forest floor   Jill Confavreux

Inspired by the abstract quality of nature and the Forest of Dean in England. Transparent glazes of gold and Payne's grey were applied and adjusted on board during different stages of the working process. Acid-free tissue paper, torn magazine pages and skeleton leaves were added to enrich the surface of the painting. Burnt hand-made paper edges were added to give the appearance of stones or fungi. Gold oil bar was scumbled over the background areas.

Acrylics, paper collage, oil bar and leaves: 600 x 300mm (24 x 12in).

Prints

Blown About Rooks   Elizabeth Nash

Inspired by rooks in autumn. The background of the trees and sunset was printed from a plate made of card, heavy duty glue and scrim. The plate was then rolled up with burnt sienna ink and printed on to damp tinted paper, using an etching press. The rooks were printed separately. The shapes were superimposed, until the desired effect was achieved.

Collograph print with oil-based ink: 500 x 400cm (20 x 16in).

Arrowana   Diane Barnes

Inspired by an Amazonian freshwater fish seen at Roundhay Park Tropical Gardens, Leeds, England. Instead of using hand tools to eliminate the lino, a solution of caustic soda and wallpaper paste was applied with a cocktail stick to eat away specific areas and shapes. Transparent medium was used extensively, building up 'glazes' of colour to suggest a watery environment.

Etched reduction linocut using oil based inks and transparent medium:
200 x 150mm (8 x 6in).

Opposite

Southern India   Diane Barnes

Inspired by travels in southern India's nature reserves and an interest in the natural world. The linocut was printed on an iron and brass nipping press. The same block was cut with hand tools and overprinted many times, working from light colours to dark. Transparent medium was used to allow overprinted colours to show through each other. Finally, the print was hand finished with gold applied to the cow horns.

Reduction linocut, oil-based inks and transparent medium: 200 x 300mm (8 x 12in).

Adders   Andrew William Seaby

Inspired by an interest in the depiction of various animals arranged in a geometrical pattern.
The first block is prepared with a dull, sandy coloured oil-based ink. A sheet of crumpled
paper is applied to the block. This produces a scribbled pattern, which is printed on very
thin white paper. The second block is printed in black, using light pressure, which gives the
snakes a stippled and scaled appearance.

Two colour linocut: 300 x 300mm (12 x 12in).

Ground Squirrels
James Williamson-Bell

Inspired by the artist's observation of these beautiful little animals, while visiting a Buddhist temple in northern China. After deciding upon the number of colours required, separate screens were made for each one. These were printed in sequence on to a wood block and the image transferred on to rice paper. After the image was built up in this way, it was signed and the artist's seal added.

Wood block transfer print: 225 x 262mm (9 x 10¹/₂in).

Rudd   Andrew William Seaby

Inspired by a shoal of rudd observed below a small weir in a French chalk stream in Normandy. A small, home-made press was used. The linocut was printed using a dark brown oil-based ink on smooth, heavy paper. When the ink was dry, the print was soaked in water and clamped in a wooden frame. It was then hand-coloured with watercolours. When the picture was completely dry it was released from the frame.

Linocut print hand-coloured with watercolour: 546 x 343mm (21 ¹/₂ x 13 ¹/₂in).

Left

Shelduck   Frans Wesselman

Inspired by watching these birds on the Welsh coast. The artist employed a combination of etched and aquatinted textures to build up colours on this multi-plate etching. Each plate was prepared to carry different shades in different areas. When superimposed in printing, these shades blended with one another, rather as in a watercolour. When carrying out this technique, arriving at the correct combinations often requires many proofs and alterations.

Etching and aquatint: 300 x 300mm (12 x 12in).

Smew - A Good Winter   Thelma K Sykes

Inspired by a drake smew on Whitemere in Shropshire, England, in the cold, clear sunlight of Christmas day. Working from field sketches and notes, white areas were cut away, and the first block was printed in black, using masking film to stop out the reflections. The birds were cut away for the second printing in the opaque blue-grey seen in the reflections. Darker grey appeared where the blue-grey overprinted the black. A second block was used to add transparent blue-green shadows on the feathers and in the reflections, creating light which illuminated the whole image.

Linocut: 145 x 120mm (5³/₄ x 4³/₄in).

Opposite

Grebe   Frans Wesselman

Inspired by a grebe in a Dutch canal. Four copper plates were printed (superimposed) in different colours. Firstly the key plate, containing the essential composition, was drawn and etched in nitric acid. It was printed, and the print was off-set on the other three plates. These were drawn and etched, guided by this printed image. They were then inked up and printed – the lightest colour first and the darkest last.

Etching and aquatint: 300 x 300mm (12 x 12in).

Textiles

Shoal of Fish   Andrew Wynne

Inspired by the artist's fascination with water, the graceful movements of fish, and reflected light and colour. The fish were painted on to Habotai silk with dye which was contained within a waxed outline. Darker shades were achieved by successive applications of wax and dye. The wax was removed from the silk completely before repeating the process, until the required interaction of line and colour was achieved by the overlapping images.

Wax resist and dye: 375 x 575mm (15 x 23in).

Stitched Jungle   Heather Blygh Lipscombe

Inspired by Marrianne North's paintings. Builder's quality cotton dust cloth does not distort or stretch, and is ideal for large pieces of stitched work. This wonderfully tactile wallhanging was stitched on to dust cloth using hand and machine embroidery. Paper and a variety of fabrics – including burnt and manipulated fabrics, were added to give texture and depth. Some of the work was padded and wired to make the leaves, seeds and berries stand out from the background.

Fabric and thread: 900 x 900mm (36 x 36in).

Index

First published in Great Britain 1996

Search Press Limited
Wellwood, North Farm Road, Tunbridge Wells, Kent TN2 3DR

Copyright © Search Press Ltd. 1996

Photography by Nigel Cheffers-Heard

Photography by Storm on pages 1 and 23

Photography by Search Press Studios on page 18

ISBN 0 85532 817 7

Printed in Spain by Elkar S. Coop.